WHERE'S GOD ON TUESDAY?

Second Edition

Marlene J. Yeo

ENDORSEMENTS

"I have observed Pastor Marlene applying God's principles in the most difficult of situations, pushing past the opinions of men to accomplish her Father's will. Through it all she functions with great passion and kindness. Pastor Marlene is most certainly "God's Girl," carrying an apostolic anointing for the 21st century!"

Pastor Rafael Najem, Senior Pastor
Community Christian Fellowship
Lowell, Massachusetts

"My friend Pastor Marlene Yeo has been one of the best kept secrets in the body of Christ. She is a woman of faith, love and compassion. I'm so glad she has decided to write a book that speaks of the journey she has been on. I believe her experiences and wisdom will speak profoundly to you and they will bring hope and healing to your soul. And if you're fourtunate, you may just catch the fire that burns deep within Marlene for God's Kingdom! Read with expectancy in your heart!"

Pastor Michael Servello Jr.
Senior Pastor
Redeemer Church
Utica, NY

"This book is a celebration of a life that draws the presence of God when Marlene is alone or in front of thousands. She and her "homies" have inspired us to press through the darkest of days.

We have had the privilege of watching

Marlene's grace as she has faced adversity, allowing God to order her steps and season her words with grace. We look forward to the coming days of walking with CCF Street Church as they continue to break yokes of bondage with humility and grace. Praise God for the victory that accompanies Marlene as she continues to allow herself to be a humble vessel of a Holy God."

Matt and Katy Stevens
Founders of Somebody Cares Baltimore and
Chain Reaction
Baltimore, Maryland

"In the context of time, there are those who are not content with the mediorcre, but emerge as change agents and history makers. Marlene Yeo is one of these. Her passionate persuit of God and to tangibly express His heart by serving the lowly to the mighty in our world is contagious.

It was with great privilege and anticipation that I read Marlene's book, "Where is God on Tuesday?" There is no doubt that the Lord has gifted her with the skill of a ready writer as she clearly communicates her journey and the Kingdom principles she has learned...often through the crucibles of experience. These experiences provided a heartfelt visual revelation into the Heartbeat of God for our communities and this generation.

There are those who write from the towers of theory, with all the statistics of information that can give us "brain freeze" or "brain overload". Then, there are the Marlene's of this world who offer us far more than just recognizing the problems of our day. She represents on who contends for authenticity in faith with action, yet offering a practical solution to the societal challenges we face in the world today.

This book will not only inspire your personal walk and journey, but it will motivate you into greater vision and hopes, expanding your faith beyond your own human capacity. You will revisit promises from the Lord for your own life that may have been forgotten, while raising the bar of expectations.

I am thankful for Marlene's life and ministry. I am proud to have her as part of our Somebody Cares global network of churches, ministries and organizations. She is a true Champion of Faith and Compassion!"

Dr. Doug Stringer
Founder/President
Somebody Cares America/International
Turning Point Ministries

"We have the privilege of knowing Marlene as mother, Pastor and friend, and we are two of her greatest fans! In each of these roles we have watched her reveal the character and the nature of Christ. We are provoked and inspired by the life of extraordinary faith, love and compassion that she lives. This book goes beyond rhetoric and theory and cuts to the heart of real life brokenness, pain and hardship and how to find God in the midst of your reality."

Darrell and Bethany Temple
Founders and Directors of Justice House of Prayer (JHOP)
Boston, Massachusetts

"Melinda and I have personally known Pastor Marlene Yeo for more than 20 years and have watched her live a life of compassion. This book is not just stories about how to do things, but is a beautiful window into the life of one of the most compassionate followers of Christ we have ever had the opportunity to call our friend. She has helped us in more ways than I can begin to express in the area of outreach, compassion ministry, and loving the lost. This book will help you to remember to keep your focus on why we do what we do and for whom we really do it. Are you ready to make a difference in your world? Then don't just read this book, live it!"

Chad Waller
Lead Pastor, VC2
Tennille, GA
CEO, Waller-Hill Publishing

FOREWORD

I thank God for the awesome testimonies and wonderful things He has done that are written this book; they are a witness of His faithfulness. I never had any intention to ever write a book until the Lord spoke several prophetic exhortations that He wanted me to do so. He also instructed me that it was not to be a book about "how to's" but about what the Lord has done in my life and ministry.

I thank Him for my husband Harry and our three incredible adult children Brandon, Bethany and Aaron and their wonderful spouses Tara, Darrell and Josephine. They have blessed us (to date) with seven of the most beautiful, brilliant, amazing grandchildren.

I want to especially thank Bethany and Darrell for their prayer support and sacrificial giving of time, energy and resources in serving the ministry of Somebody Cares N.E. and launching of (CCF Haverhill) Community Christian Fellowship. I couldn't have done it without them. Although they are both missed by the entire staff of CCF we are all so proud of them and the ministry they founded and direct Justice House of Prayer and the church they planted and pastor Hilltop Church in Cambridge, Massachusetts.

I am grateful to God for the wisdom I have received from the men of God that have invested their lives in mentoring me. I am modeling in ministry today what they have taught me. In order of when I met them Pastor Mike Servello, Sr. and Pastor Mike Servello, Jr. Dr. Doug Stringer and Pastor Rafael Najem. Their investment in my life has not been in vain; great is their reward in heaven.

My deepest gratitude to the Lord for the servant leaders that have laid down their life to that serve in Somebody Cares New England and helped to plant Community Christian Fellowship (CCF) Haverhill. I have never served with a more faithful, dedicated, caring group of people in my whole life. Although we are an extremely diverse group (praise the Lord) our love for God, people and the mission "taking the love and power of Christ to the streets" has given us the strength to face every challenge together.

Thank you Peggy Foley, John and Sandy Furtado and family, Jeff and Letriah Masters and family, Kevin and Reggie Moriarty, George and Connie Plouffe and family, Lori Jane Simmer, Sue Quaranta and Pastor Rafael Najem.

TABLE OF CONTENTS

INTRODUCTION

"Where is God on Tuesday?" was never a title I would have chosen for a book. The title became apparent one day while speaking at the Somebody Cares America/International Summit in Houston, Texas. I made the comment, "Isn't it amazing that on Sunday we can be so encouraged by the worship, the message and prophetic revelation we receive, yet on Monday when asked how was service and what did the Lord speak we draw a blank having difficulty remembering. The noise of this life has a way of drowning out what we experienced just one day before and two days later we find ourselves asking, "Where is God on Tuesday?" After speaking I sat down next to my friend Katy Stevens, who wrote on a napkin, what a great name for a book, "Where is God on Tuesday?" directly following Katy's comments Dr. Stuart Quartemont came to me and said, "While you were speaking the Lord impressed me to tell you, He wants you to write a book. Not about "how to (s)" but a testimony of what the Lord has done in your life.

So...here it is...my first book, written for all the "crazies" who are in love with Jesus. Those people who want to make a difference in this messed up world but find themselves limited in resources, time and skill to accomplish much more than making a living just to survive and raising a family.

It is written for all the nameless, faceless ones, I call the "little people" who have a dream to make a difference in this short lifetime. Those who are hoping that someday.... just maybe, somebody out there will believe in what the Lord has called them to do and help them to do it.

If that is you I have a word of wisdom for you, quit looking for the big somebody to give you the big break, to offer the big opportunity, or the big whatever! Just begin obeying God right where you are, using just what you have. When you look at what others have, their accomplishments, their influence, their resources it only produces discouragement, jealousy and fear. Looking at others will render you useless where you are and powerless to move forward.

God is the one who opens doors that no man can shut.
(Revelations 3:8)

He elevates one and sets down another.
(Psalm 75:2-7)

What is done and spoken in the dark place will be shouted from the housetop.
(Luke 12:2-4)

He is the Faithful and Just One and He will reward openly that which is done in His name in secret.
(Matthew 6:4)

If we really believe what the Lord speaks to us we must allow the Holy Spirit to make us willing to live our lives before the Him in the hidden place. No kudos, no praise, no pay, no glory, no favors, even when it seems we are destined for defeat, difficulty and disappointment. Suddenly one day God will open the gates that once confined you. You will pass through the narrow passageway into the new place He has for you, Micah 2:13 says,

"I will go before you and I will lead you in. He is the breaker; He breaks in to break you out!"

We are like the nameless, faceless man that God used in Ecclesiastes 9:15:

Now there was found in the city a poor wise man, and he by his wisdom delivered the city. Yet no one remembered that same poor man.

We may never receive the credit, fame or fortune we think we deserve in this life. But we must live life knowing that in eternity the rewards of faithfulness are given to those who obeyed what God spoke and were good stewards with what He gave them.

They, whoever they are, may never know the sacrifices you made, but God knows. He knows every act of kindness, every tear shed for those in need of the Savior, every prayer prayed in faith and every hand extended in love to those in need. He is crazy in love with you and me and He's dancing a happy dance over those who serve Him with a cheerful and willing heart!

In the words of Ann Kimmel, "I'm just an ordinary girl with an extraordinary God."

This book is about my journey, as an ordinary person fulfilling the purposes of God for my life in my generation. I have learned to press through when it feels like God is a galaxy away and to trust that He will do what He promised and finish what He started. My prayer for you, as you read this book is that you will be encouraged to press into His destiny for you regardless of the obstacles, the trials and the pain.

This book is not a deep theological exegesis, it's just real, raw, relevant documentary of my journey from brokenness to wholeness and from a victim to victor in Christ. As I begin writing I must warn you my honesty may offend you and my silly humor my cause you to think I am not doctrinally sound. To the first

I say, forgiveness is a beautiful thing and to the latter I say, "Oh well!" Try as I might to behave, I have a feeling my personality will leak through the pages of this book.

1. HOME IS WHERE THE HURT IS

I was raised in a typical (not so) Christian American home. My family attended church on the expected occasions such as Easter and Christmas Eve. I never owned a bible or heard anyone in our family talk about God, the name of Jesus Christ was heard only when used as slang or swear.

I am the oldest of three with two younger brothers. Born in 1952 to alcoholic parents; although they loved each other they could not get along. Their miserable marriage ended in divorce after 19 years. My mother battled mental illness and my Dad was a workaholic. Being at work and away from Mom was a welcomed relief. Their relationship was extremely strained and very stressful. They often had verbally aggressive arguments that would on occasion become combative waking us kids up.

Because of the unrest in our home we had relational and behavioral issues that provoked our parents who were unskilled in managing their own behavior and emotions. Often we experienced excessive spankings out of their frustrations instead of discipline with instruction. The results of both neglect and abuse developed a shame base character in us. We all ended up to some degree acting out socially, morally and relationally destructive lifestyles.

Most of the memories of life in our family were painful and left deep wounds on my self image. I have no memory of my parents reading me a book, playing with me or tucking me in bed. I never felt protected, celebrated or cared for. My brothers and I have a deep love for each other although since my salvation experience we have very different life styles.

17

Even though we don't agree about God or the bible it does not change the bond of love and respect we have for one another.

My childhood was laced with fear. One of the repeated dreams I had when I was very young and still in my crib was the face of a strange man standing over my bed with a very long thick rope. He would tie it to one corner and wind it around my bed up to the ceiling (my crib was under a slant roof). It felt like I was being buried alive. From an early age I felt uncomfortable in my own skin, I didn't like who I was, what I looked like or my personality. At the core of my being was self- rejection.

My Mom used to say "for God's sake can you sit still for one minute." When the Madagascar movie came out I thought they stole my theme song, "we like to move it, move it". Standing or sitting still to me was a torturous form of punishment to my sanguine personality. My Mom on the other hand was a melancholy book worm who enjoyed quiet and solitude.

At the age of twelve I remember one night running from my home to find refuge at a friend's house. My friends mixed my first drink and gave me my first cigarette. As the years progressed drinking was a daily part of my life. I used it to self medicate my pain. When I was drinking it gave me a strange sense of joy, false sense of peace and distorted sense of courage. But the reality is it opened doors to more confusion, fear, abuse and addiction.

My teenage years up until I met the Lord at age 26 spiraled out of control. Without a foundation or a compass I continually made bad choices. My mentality was like the song says, "all we are is dust in the wind". I didn't care about much of anything except doing what I wanted, when I wanted and with whom I wanted. As the years passed I became more and more self -conscious, self- absorbed and self -centered.

I never had a bond with my mother; in her last years of life I had the privileged of being her caregiver in my home for almost two years. As difficult as that was I knew it was an opportunity to share God's love with her. The Lord opened her heart and she asked for forgiveness although at that time refused to give forgiveness to my father. When she died the only emotion I felt was sadness for her and the painful life she lived; she never found happiness. My hope is that before she passed that she finally let go of her bitterness and forgave my father.

Although I believe my Dad loved me he had a difficult time expressing it. Most of his life was spent working hard for a living so that our basic needs were met. From the time my parents divorced when I was 18 years old he had several girlfriends, wives and stepchildren that consumed his life.

In his elder years his health failed miserably, because of that he was not involved with women which gave opportunity for us to connect relationally. During one of my visits with him in Florida I was giving him a foot soak, I felt in my heart to wash his feet and pray for him. He wept as I shared with him how much I loved him and I knew he had done the best he knew how to raise us kids amidst the difficult life that we lived. I offered to pray with him to receive the love of Christ and he accepted with great joy as he experienced the peace and presence of God and forgiveness.

Have you ever been angry with God for allowing you to be born in your family? For giving you the job you feel mistreated at, for that difficult neighbor you live next door to, for planting you in a church where you feel misunderstood? I can relate, and I am here to tell you, although He is not the author of the madness, He has a purpose in it all!

*And we know that all things work togeth-
er for good to those who love God, to those
who are the called according to His purpose.*
- Romans 8:28

*"Before I formed you in the womb I knew
you, before you were born I set you apart; I appointed you as a prophet to the nations."*
- Jeremiah 1:5

It took many years of prayer and coun-
seling from the word of God before I experienced healing of the wounded emotions that
were once my constant companion. Now, on
this side of my journey, ministering to the people that God has called me to I can see the purpose for everything He has allowed to touch my
life.

The children of Israel were instructed to
look at the serpent that Moses lifted up in the
wilderness. As they looked at the very thing that
bit them they were healed. The areas of my life
that had been wounded by the enemy, although
his purpose was to destroy my life, are the very
areas that God has anointed me to bring healing to others.

2. THANK GOD FOR GOD

I have a very dear friend named Janice who would witness to me about God's heart for me and how He sent His Son to demonstrate His love. I would often reject her efforts because I found it difficult to believe that He existed and that He even cared. My world of pain was more real to me than God was.

She was not moved by my verbal rejection of her efforts and continued to pray for me. Finally late one night in January 1977 while channel surfing I came across a Christian TV show. The man hosting the show shared the truth about God's love then invited viewers to pray and accept Jesus as their Lord and Savior. I responded with my whole heart as tears poured down my cheeks I experienced real peace for the first time in my life.

I have often wished my testimony was...and then.....bam.....everything suddenly changed.....but it didn't. But what I can say is that as I applied the principles of truth found in the word of God and as I chose to remain in Him that through prayer, obedience and the help of the Holy Spirit He has changed every area of my life.

I am a new creature in Christ, old things have passed away and all things have become new.

II Corinthians 5:17

Until I found a local church to attend I would travel into Boston to a Catholic charismatic healing service with some friends from work. It was there that I experienced my first miraculous healing; I had chronic psoriasis on my hands and feet. Ashamed of the ugliness of my hands I had difficulty exchanging money with a cashier or shaking hands. My

21

bloody, cracked, oozing flesh looked to me like leprosy. I was treated with medication and ointments of which never did any good because it was neurological in nature.

On the second morning after having received prayer the skin on my hands and feet were like that of a baby; clean, clear and brand new! My faith in God sky rocketed to new heights. Not only did He forgive my sins, saved me from the path of destruction, mended my broken heart, He healed my body and my jangled nervous system. Go figure, this God that I know and love wants our messed up life in exchange for His joy and peace!

It is amazing to me how we, as the created ones, fight against the Creator resisting His gift of new life and peace. We deceive ourselves thinking that our bondage and sin are really life and happiness. All I can say is "thank God for God", as my friend Peggy says. He paid a high price, the life and blood of His sinless Son in exchange for depraved, lost humanity. I am forever grateful and amazed that He broke through into my prison and captured my heart with His love!

I have walked with the Lord since January 1977 and I have seen multitudes of people come to a saving knowledge of Christ and experienced amazing breakthroughs, healing and freedom. The word speaks about our journey with Christ as being a daily walk, taking up our cross and denying self. Although many are called there are not as many who remain on the pathway to holiness and allow the Holy Spirit's work of transformation. Jesus said in Matthew 7:14:

"Narrow is the gate and difficult is the way which leads to life, and there are few who find it."

Many allow the difficulties, trials, temptations and cares of life as spoken in Matthew 13:18-23 to choke out and scorch the seed of faith. It is a difficult journey, one of dying to self and choosing His ways and thoughts over our own. Unfortunately many get discouraged and give up along the way.

I will be writing about some of the challenges that God has allowed to cross my path. I use the word cross....because each challenge was a cross road of opportunity that God used to bring me to a greater death of self and a greater revelation of Him. Because of His amazing grace I am not angry or bitter about what He has allowed to fashion my life. As Joseph said in Genesis 45: 7-8:

*"God has sent me before you to preserve posterity for you in the earth and to save your lives by a great deliverance. So it was not you who sent me here, **BUT** God..."*

As previously stated; Romans 8:28 He worked all things together for my good because; my love for Him was greater than my desire for comfort. I choose to remain while He continues the work preparing me to receive His promises. I have had the opportunity to walk with some wonderful people who loved God, some of whom are mentioned in this book (whose names may be changed). Some of them stopped making the choice to abide in His grace until they got to enjoy the sweet fruit that is produced out of adversity.

3. SERVING OPEN DOORS

I remember as, a young believer, attending my first conference and asking the Lord what He wanted me to do to serve Him. Before the end of the weekend, He directed me to Ecclesiastes 9:10,

"What ever your hand finds to do, do [it] with your might; for [there is] no work or device or knowledge or wisdom in the grave where you are going."

I have known many that get stuck in having to know their gift and calling before they begin to serve the Lord. When I would read about the gifts of the Holy Spirit I had a hard time trying to identify what mine were. So this verse was a welcomed relief. It was simple, do what needed to be done with all my heart.

Although I had heard many teachings about the gifts it was years before I received personal revelation regarding what mine were. I am glad the Lord hasn't allowed things to come easy, it has taught me to trust and obey Him, even when I don't "get it." It has taught me to serve Him because of who He is and not for the gifts He gives or for what He does for me.

There are many who strive to use their spiritual gift on a platform to be seen by men but have not learned the principal of serving in the hidden place and that serving is the open door that will make room for your gift. To quote an old friend of mine the Big 'O' who would say, "You serve your way to your purpose." and the little Yeo (me) adding, "And when you find your purpose, keep serving".

Whenever there was a church clean-up scheduled, I would show up ready to work. When trash was on the floor, I picked it up. When the paper rolls were empty, I would refill it.

I enjoyed making God's house clean and orderly. I have found over the years serving in church clean up and prayer gatherings are two areas that people feel least "called to".

I remember an Elder in the church I was attending say to me, "It's just a matter of time before you will be in leadership; you take care of God's stuff as if it were your own." As my children grew, I served in whatever area of ministry they were in, nursery, kid's church and VBS. When my kids were teens I served as the youth minister for ten years and then I served during their young adult years as an Associate Pastor.

It is a wonderful thing when the Lord works the principle of serving in your life. You never have to try hard to do it...it's just a part of who you are and you enjoy serving knowing that it brings Him and others great joy.

God is looking for servant leaders. I was powerfully impacted by the messages Pastor Bill Wilson of Metro Ministries preached. One of the messages taken from I Chronicles 13 and 15 - David chose the home of Obed-Edom to keep the ark of the presence of God for three months. As you read in chapter 15, Obed-Edom was a servant in the house of the Lord; he did whatever was needed to be done. Servants are trusted to be the keepers of the ark of His presence.

My heart's cry is, "Lord, let me be a carrier of Your presence, Let Your peace and power be real to a lost and dying world; let them see Christ living in me. I choose not to let the disappointment, pain and difficulty of life render me useless; but through Your grace I would always rise above to be better skilled and more useful through each challenge or loss.

Being a servant isn't something you start out as and grow into leadership; the Son of Man was the greatest Servant Leader of humanity, He came not to be served but to serve. He stripped Himself of His garments, gird Himself with a towel and washed their feet.

"So when He had washed their feet, taken His garments, and sat down again, He said to them, "Do you know what I have done to you? You call Me Teacher and Lord, and you say well, for [so] I am. If I then, [your] Lord and Teacher, have washed your feet, you also ought to wash one another's feet. For I have given you an example, that you should do as I have done to you. Most assuredly, I say to you, a servant is not greater than his master; nor is he who is sent greater than he who sent him. If you know these things, blessed are you if you do them."
- John 13:12-17

Over the years many have asked me the question "How is it that you have been able to step into the prophetic promises that God has given to you, many have a calling but few have actually stepped into their destiny?" The answer is very simple although very difficult:

•   Prayer - pray and keep on praying-declaring those things that are not as though they were. Choosing not to be controlled by what is but believe what God has said.

•   Obey - whatever the Lord speaks and makes real to you from His word just do it! You may not be so skilled, so good or even so great at it...so what, just do it!

•   Remain - regardless of the obstacles and challenges, stay put, don't run.

•   Trust - when others and even your own

doubts scream, "Why can't you just be normal? Why do you care so much? You're really not called to do this, if you were, it would be easier".

- Press - keep pushing, don't give in or give up!! After having done all you know to do... stand!

- Character – it isn't what men say about you, it's what angels know about you. To God and thine own self be true. Everyone will have an opinion about you. One day they call you a hero the next day you're a zero. Don't let public opinion move you. Don't take credit for what works or blame for what doesn't. Let success and failure be a tool to mold you into Christ likeness.

- Honor those that God puts in your life that make you look good. Give credit where credit is due. Don't act smarter than you are.

- Rest along the way - take time out to be renewed and refreshed. It may take 5-10-20 or 30 years before you see the fruit of your labors. You're in it for the long haul, until death do us part, there is no plan B. Sometimes we end up trying too hard...but I have found the more I rest in Him, the better things works out. He loves to reveal Himself through impossible situations.

- Give Him thanks in and through all things. It keeps you out of the prison house of self pity and keeps your eyes fixed on the prize!

4. GOD HAS A DREAM

Often I have prayed according to Joel 2:28; that God would give me dreams and visions. It wasn't until August 1998 while attending a compassion conference in Utica, NY at Mt. Zion Ministries (renamed Redeemer Church) that I realized God has a dream. His dream is for His church to tell the whole world of His love, that His body would love one another and show His compassion and mercy to all and that the church would be His house of prayer for all nations. God invites us to be a part of making His dream come to pass. None of us can reach the "whole world" but we can begin with our own family, neighborhood, school, job and city. His dream is that His bride, the church, would be the tangible presence of His love demonstrated in the part of the world we live in (Matt. 22:37-39).

One of the guest speakers at the Utica conference was Pastor Harold Caballeros from Guatemala. I heard his testimony how the Lord brought transformation to his city on the first Transformation DVD produced by sentinel group (www.glowtorch.org). While at the conference the Lord gripped my heart. For three days my nose was in the carpet repenting for not having His heart for people. I cried out for Him to send me as a "sent one" wherever He wanted to go.

God's dream for His kids is not only that they love one another but that they actually learn to "get along".

"A new commandment I give to you, that you love one another; as I have loved you, that you also love one another. By this all will know that you are My disciples, if you have love for one another."

- John 13:34-35

"That they all may be one, as You, Father, [are] in Me, and I in You; that they also may be one in Us, that the world may believe that You sent Me."

- John 17:21

Jesus said the two greatest commandments are to love the Lord with all your heart and your neighbor as yourself. Who is my neighbor you ask?....why it's your neighbor! The one standing, sitting, eating, sleeping, working and walking next to you right now! God wants to answer the prayer Jesus prayed for His disciples, He is waiting for us to choose to walk in love. How His heart is grieved when His children contend and strive with one another. We have been a poor witness to the world. It is time to build bridges, put aside foolish pride, humble ourselves and reach out to our brothers and sisters. We must come together because of Jesus, for the sake of the lost and love our cities together.

God dreams of a day when the church returns to her calling as a "house of prayer". Isaiah 56:7 and Mark 11:17 says, My house shall be called a house of prayer for all Nations. The thought of starting a house of prayer never entered my mind until I went to Herrnhut, Germany and climbed the stairs of the Moravian prayer tower. It was during a 10 day trip to Europe with my brother Marland and my daughter Bethany. I had the once in a lifetime opportunity to spend two days in Herrnhut where Count Zinzendorf gave His life as a prayer compassion missionary. The community of believers experienced an outpouring of the Holy Spirit that began a prayer movement of 24/7 that endured over 125 years.

As I stood on top of the prayer tower looking out across the beautiful land of Germany I felt the presence of the Lord and began to sob for America. My heart cried out, "Lord do in America what you have done here in Germany, birth 24/7 prayer in every city across the nation. Bring the church of Jesus Christ together once again to pray for the wellbeing of her cities. America needs a move of the Holy Spirit."

When I returned home from Germany I gathered the leadership team together and shared with them the call I felt from the Lord to birth a house of prayer. We fasted and prayed for 21 days seeking the Lord for His anointing to launch it. At the end of the three weeks we invited Jeff Marks, an apostolic prayer intercessor, a father in the faith. Jeff has labored in prayer for New England, America and the nations for decades. In November 2007 we began our humble beginnings believing God to establish His tower of prayer here in Haverhill.

5. DOWN IS UP

After that powerful encounter with the Lord in Utica I thought I would then be catapulted forward into my destiny.....but after receiving revelation of His dream I plummeted to the depths of despair, which marked one of my many trips to what I jokingly refer to as the "bowels of hell". My life in ministry up until that point had been pretty normal, sane and predictable, that was now forever gone.

My relationships, ministry, finances and home suffered (what I considered) unbearable losses. The Lord used that painful period of about three years to transition me out of the church I had served in for over 20 years, of which I have to say I did not handle with much emotional maturity or great skill. I had never been through such an experience of brokenness in ministry before.

When Joseph received his dreams from God the first place he experienced challenge was with his closest relationships. It is evident from scripture and my own experience that misunderstanding, jealousy and fear are assigned to escort you to your new assignments from God. In addition to the emotional upheaval of losing the comforts of home, everything Joseph knew was taken from him. Although he served wherever God allowed him to go, he was accused of wrong behavior even though innocent.

It is one thing to read about the life of Joseph it is another to walk a mile in his moccasin (so to speak) and gain understanding of the process the Lord brings us through. After receiving revelation from His word you are baptized into the furnace of affliction. If your responses are right you will not only survive the pain from the challenges but also learn to thrive in spite of them, finally arriving at the joy of seeing the promise come to pass as written in Genesis chapters 37-50.

As we are advancing forward into our destiny we often we find ourselves in a descent downward. In my downward spiral I was experiencing emotions of intense fear and great confusion, my carnal thoughts were, "I must have done something terribly wrong." "If this is how God treats His favorites, how do I get off His favorite list? It felt like "the gods" must be angry and they're trying to kill me!

It is during those times of testing God seems to be distant and silent giving no understanding of what is happening. But I have learned to embrace those dark times as the crucible that God uses to reveal the thoughts and intents of my own heart and attitude.

The words of the LORD [are] pure words, [Like] silver tried in a furnace of earth, purified seven times.
(Psalm 12:6)

In preparing us to receive His promises, He allows our faith to be tried in the furnace of the earth (the deepest place of our soul). We don't know who we really are or what is lodged deep inside of us, only the Lord knows the secret thoughts and intentions of the heart. Just like Peter, Jesus allowed him to walk through the pain of denying the Lord which exposed what was in Peter's heart to himself.

Jesus prayed for him that once he was restored he would strengthen the brethren. Peter went from the one who knew everything and the Lord knowing nothing, to the one who knew nothing and the Lord knowing everything (Matt. 26:35 and John 21:17). Those places in us must be revealed to be healed to make us ready for our destiny.

> *Now this, "He ascended"--what does it mean but that He also first descended into the lower parts of the earth?*
>
> - Ephesians 4:9

As we surrender to Him it is only God that can take the horrible experiences of life, wash them with His blood and makes us better and not bitter.

Another passage Pastor Bill Wilson preached from was Judges 20:15-16. The tribe of Benjamin had an army of 700 select men who were left handed warriors; they were extremely skilled with their left hand. Every one of them could sling a stone at a hair's breadth and not miss their target.

Left handed people were considered the outcasts, the un-desirables. Where do 700 left handed men of war come from? Could it be they had been in previous battles, suffered the loss of right hand use, and were retrained to use their left hand to actually become better because of their disability? The Bible is full of stories about fragile, weak human beings- men, women and young ones who were the least, the last and the lost who failed miserably. God delights in choosing them as the very ones to accomplish His purposes through. The wounded ones who have been healed seem to be a secret weapon God uses to break through enemy lines with His love!

Has there been a time in your life when you received a dream or a word from God revealing what He called you to do? Did it spark a burning desire to serve Him but as the Lord allowed the testing and pain to come you rolled over like the disciples in the garden and went to sleep. It's time to shake off the slumber of disappointment and discouragement shake off the pain like Paul shook off the serpent from his arm at the coal fire in Malta. It's time to give it up, give it over and give in to His process to perfect you. Once you do, you will be amazed as the Lord does miracles in you, for you, around you and through you!

6. IF THE BURDEN IS LIGHT, HOW COME MY BACK HURTS?

"For My yoke [is] easy and My burden is light."

(Matthew 11:30)

I thought when we receive a burden from the Lord it meant it was going to be easy as in "a piece of cake" like "no sweat".....yah, right? The definition of burden is to load heavily, oppressively; trouble. That which is borne with difficulty; obligation; the burden of leadership, weigh down, saddle, try, afflict, perturb, plague, grieve, vex, a load of any kind, a severe task (Ex. 2:11), a difficult duty, requiring effort (Ex. 18:22).

When I received His burden, to live as a prayer compassion missionary sent to Haverhill, Massachusetts, not only was my heart broken with compassion for people; but I have a new understanding of the term "blood, sweat and tears". Part of my assignment has been to bring reform to the Christian community mindset. I have found that in the western church there is a false ideology regarding prayer and missions. There is a stronghold in the mind and heart of many believers.

You can hear the mindsets weaved through out many conversations regarding prayer and missions, it sounds like, "Not everyone is called to pray for their city and missions are for those nations that need it, not here in America. We are already a Christian nation besides we have education, doctors and the best welfare system in the world".

Little did I know after returning home

37

from that conference in 1998 how much everything was about to change. It was during that time that I was serving as the Youth Minister in my local church. I began to share the burden God had ruined me with, His heart for those right here on the streets of Haverhill, Massachusetts... right here in America.

But you shall receive power when the Holy Spirit comes upon you; and you shall be witnesses to Me in Jerusalem, in all of Judea and Samaria and to the end of the earth.
(Acts 1:8)

God had called, commissioned and commanded me to go to my Jerusalem, Haverhill.

I announced to the youth ministry team and young people, "We will never return to business as usual, the ministry now has a missions focus." We began a three month intensive teaching and training the youth to be missionaries to their schools, their neighborhood, at their jobs and we took them to the streets.

The first outreach was a Block Party July 1999 in downtown Haverhill at GAR Park. I invited a youth minister friend of mine from Michigan; he brought his leadership staff, youth ministry team leaders, their worship band and drama team of about 30 people. We had an amazing day of music, ministry, food and fun; we fed over 500 people that day.

Those attending the Block Party were the distressed population of single moms, children, youth, elderly and homeless. I was impacted by their grateful hearts even through the look of desperation in their eyes. I knew from that moment that the Lord had called me not to just do outreaches...but to be the outreach as a means that God was using to draw the people that He wanted us to show His love and kindness to.

From the July outreach through December the youth prepared for the next opportunity to share the love of Jesus with those in distress. We planned a Christmas party serving dinner for the homeless instead of a "Yankee swap" for each other. I challenged the youth to save their money and even consider asking their parents for up to half of the money they would normally spend on their gifts and allow them to buy new gifts for the homeless to give out on Christmas day. Although the outreach was presented as an option for the youth and the families that wanted to be involved it was a challenging time for all. As the time grew closer mindsets, fears and insecurities were exposed. Some parents were annoyed feeling it was a disruption to "the family tradition" for their child to be involved with an outreach on Christmas day. Some expressed fear for their kids, after all the homeless were "dangerous people". But the saddest mindset of all was "how can you do that to us, it's a holy day for families?"

REALLY people.....my response to them, "What would Jesus be found doing on Christmas Day? The greatest gift we could give Him is to share His love with the forgotten ones." On that first Christmas day about 12 youth and 8 adults went to the homeless shelter with me and experienced something that none of us had ever experienced before. The presence of Jesus was tangible. There were tears of joy from all who were present as we shared a meal, the love of Christ, the good news of the gospel and gifts for each person.

One woman, who was known as the worst drunk in Haverhill, had tried to strangle a young man, who was a known drug user, the day before Christmas. He had punched her in the face trying to defend himself. His neck was a raw, bloody mess and she looked like a raccoon. After I shared about the greatest Christmas gift of all, Jesus, she received His love and forgiveness. Immediately she went over to the man she tried to strangle as they wept together giving and receiving forgiveness.

One father, who had come with his teenage children to protect them from the "evil people" in the shelter said to me as they left, "This was the best Christmas I have ever had in my life! I experienced what Christmas is all about; it's giving freely the love of Christ to those He died for. I came here thinking I needed to protect my kids, but God's plan was to wreck my heart with His compassion for people who need His love"

That Christmas Day in 1999 began the tradition of serving the community on the national holidays, Thanksgiving, Christmas and New Years breakfast and lunch. Our doors were open from 7 am-4 pm, providing day shelter, clothing, and a tractor trailer truck of groceries and personal care products, music, prizes and most important an atmosphere of love, caring and sharing.

Over the years hundreds of testimonies were, "If it wasn't for Somebody Cares I would have no one to be with for the holidays, you are my family and being here with all of you is what I look forward to every year." Many addicts and alcoholics have thanked us for giving them a reason not to use on that day, saying, "I used to have to get wasted to escape the loneliness on the holidays, thanks for giving me a reason to be sober!

The pain and difficulty these precious people endure is beyond words. Yes, many of them have made bad choices thus the state of despair they live in. But most of them have been sinned against by others when they were small children and teens and have been emotionally crippled beyond human repair. Outside of God's miraculous intervention of a miracle their only hope is finding the right medication to help them cope and just exsist. Because of the mir-

40

acles Christ has done in my life, I know nothing is impossible with God! Because of what I have experienced, I have the faith to believe that He is able to rescue those in the gutter most and raise them up to the uttermost!

Although being called to the mission of loving the least, the last, the lost, the little and the lonely is a challenging one it has also been a great joy and a delight to serve them. I remember one man at our Christmas day outreach looking over the gift table where each guest could choose a gift for themselves and wrap a gift for someone they love. He was homeless, distressed, depressed and lonely. His remark was, "Nobody cares about me on Christmas day or any other day!" I was able to encourage him that the very reason we were there offering a day of shelter, food, fun, prayer and resources was because Jesus loved and cared for him. I shared with him that everything we did on that day was God demonstrating His love through us just for him.

His eyes filled with tears as we looked for his gift. At the end of the day he came to me saying, "I have never felt what I experienced here today, you gave me the gift of love and peace". He left that afternoon to go back into the shelter knowing that Jesus loves him.

That is the reward for the blood, sweat and tears; when you get to be the donkey God uses to carry His presence into your Jerusalem; and you have the privilege of watching Him reveal His love to hurting people and seeing them touched by His presence through you!

In June of 2002 I met a very special man named Dr. Doug Stringer. A mutual friend of ours Helena Wang kept encouraging me to meet him. She told me the story of when he was 25 years of age he started taking a group of Christian young people out to the streets of Houston, TX in the middle of the night as the

41

bars would close. They passed out "Somebody Cares" business cards with 24 hour phone # to the runaways, addicts, prostitutes, and anyone in distress. Today the ministry of Somebody Cares America/ International (www.somebody-cares.org) is not only in multiple cities through out the USA but also in several nations. God is using SCA/SC Int'l as first responders in disasters across the globe.

Helena tried on several occasions to arrange a conversation but I was pretty good at dodging them. I felt extremely insecure, I compared the magnitude of Doug's ministry to the little outreaches I was doing in Haverhill and felt I would be a waste of the man's time. Then finally the Lord cornered me and I had lunch with Doug, Helena and my daughter Bethany. He asked me about the ministry that I was doing in Haverhill. As I shared my passion for Jesus and the compassion He put in my heart for the people tears flooded my salad and I could hardly eat. I told him how my heart was burdened ever since I had seen the Transformation DVD and that something happened to me that I couldn't explain.

I apologized to him for being so emotional; I explained that when I shared my passion I often got blubbery. As Doug listened he looked at me wide eyed, my thoughts raced, "This guy thinks I am a cuckoo head." But his response was very comforting; he gave language to the emotions I felt as he spoke in his very calm Asian manner and said, "You are carrying a burden from the Lord for your city; He has raised you up as a woman of peace. I would like to come to your city and meet the people you serve". What?..... this man who was known across the globe for prayer and the work of compassion wants to come to my city?

Doug paid his own way to come in November of 2002, he ministered in two churches and met with 5 Pastors to share the vision of SCA. We walked the streets of the city of Haverhill and I introduced him to my homies at the day shelter. During his visit I brought Doug to the abandoned campus of the former Bradford College that was for sale. It had originally been founded as a private Christian school for girls known as Bradford Christian Academy. One of the first missionaries to leave American soil graduated from the school, Ann Haseltine, who married Adoniram Judson. As Doug stood there on the property he said, "I believe the Lord wants to re-dig the wells here on this campus and send out missionaries once again from this place that will touch the four corners of the world. Gather the intercessors together and pray it through and watch what the Lord will do!"

Yes sir! We did just that, we called out to intercessors throughout New England and we began to walk the property and call those things that were not as though they were. Not only did we pray regularly on the campus we also did prayer walks through-out the city as the Lord would reveal the areas He wanted us to go. Doug felt there was a DNA for city transformation here in Haverhill and said, "As you wash the feet of the poor it touches the heart of the Father and opens the heavens for His blessing over a city and His presence will transforms lives.

As we cried out for God to once again fill the desecrated, abandoned campus with His presence and for His intended purposes to come to pass...He did just that. Northpoint bible college, formerly Zion Bible college of Barrington, RI was seeking the Lord for His perfect will for them. He sent them on the wings of a financial miracle to Haverhill, Massachusetts provided by Hobby Lobby, to the campus we were praying on. Hooray for God! Doug Stringer's word of wisdom from the Holy Spirit many years ago was, "find the will of God, serve it and watch what He does!

43

By March 2003 Somebody Cares New England was incorporated and licensed under Somebody Cares America/Int'l. SCNE is not a para church organization that does humanitarian deeds; it is a living organism made up of people who are praying for the transformation of individuals and cities, caring through meeting practical needs and sharing the good news of God's love. Prior to becoming a Somebody Cares Chapter we did outreaches for several years and were a blessing to the people we served. But since become a Somebody Cares chapter we have become a relational net in 5 cities, believers from over 10 denominations and three synagogues serve at the holiday outreaches and block parties and hundreds of volunteers serve from all walks of life.

Whenever you put your hand to the plow it stirs up a hornets nest in the spirit realm. The enemy doesn't care how much you know his concern is when you step out in faith to put into practice what you know.

But it so happened, when Sanballat heard that we were rebuilding the wall, that he was furious and very indignant, and mocked the Jews.
- Nehemiah 4:1

The enemy stirred up contention, strife, jealousy and gossip among pastors that created such calamity and confusion that I found myself emotionally wrestling not wanting to be a part of Somebody Cares or interceding for the re-digging of the missions well. The backlash of accusation and slander continued for several years . One pastor spoke publicly about the ministry of Somebody Cares and would tell anyone he spoke to both in and out of his church not to be involved because I was a woman in rebellion.

Several years ago for the National Day

44

of Prayer (NDP) I had been invited to lead the prayer segment for unity in the churches, that is until another pastor in the city found out I was scheduled to speak. He told the coordinator to remove me because of accusations he had heard about me. She was mortified when she called to un-invite me. I humbled myself that day and chose to go and pray with my brothers and sisters in Christ, I was not going to allow the accusation to keep me from praying and rob me.

Several years later for the (NDP) Somebody Cares New England was asked to co-chair with Common Ground Ministries. The Lord has a way of turning things around, the same woman who had told me I couldn't participate several years earlier came up to me to express her gratitude to the Lord for vindicating me, her words were, "I am so sorry, I knew you were all about unity but I couldn't defend you, I am so glad the Lord did!" I had the joy of telling her how God used it to do a work of humility in me and I didn't blame her or her pastor because my steps are ordered of the Lord!

I have learned walking through the valleys to cast my burden upon the Lord, for He cares for me. His burden then becomes light when He is invited to carry it with you.

7. THESE PEOPLE ARE YOUR PEOPLE

Time and again I have to be reminded; these are God's people, not mine.

I chuckle at the conversation between God and Moses regarding the children of Israel that I like to paraphrase, "God do something with "Your" people and God says to Moses, you get down off the mountain and you do something with "your" people!"

Many times my heart has cried in intercession not only for the people that I serve in the inner city as a minister of reconciliation but also for the people of God who "claim to" have knowledge of the word of the Lord.

At times I have found myself annoyed with God for not doing what I think He should to bring about justice for those I serve as well as for myself. When the outreaches in Haverhill first began there was tremendous excitement in the church...this was the "new thing" that got everyone revved up, it was fun and exciting. Often times when a ministry is birthed, just like a new baby, everyone feels called to join what's happening when in reality they are just coming to check it out.

Not so many who feel called are willing to take the night feedings or change the messy diapers. The majority wants to show up the day of the party to serve after the hard work of raising the funds, gathering the resources and all the preparations are done. Then when the party is over volunteers disappear rather quickly because very few feel "called" to the ministry of clean up. After all they came in their party pants and don't want to get dirty.

During the second year of outreaches there arose some "concern" too many of the church members had been serving the city reaching mission instead of being involved in areas of ministry in the church. There were discussions how this was now causing a division (two different visions) because I was now drawing church members away from the mission statement of the church which was building a "Charismatic Family Church" it was beginning to look more like an "Inner City Missions Church". The city of Haverhill was not only a half an hour away from the little suburban church I was attending but also across the boarder in another state. We were given use of a 15 passenger van to transport the "inner city folks" to the church service on Sunday. It was creating a bit of a problem; "city issues" were now present in a white suburbia church, what was God thinking?

I found myself having to navigate this very difficult situation. I loved my church and believed in submitting to my leaders yet I had this mandate and mission from God that seemed to be creating problems for not only me but the church as well. I would vent at God how unfair all this was, after all I didn't sign up for this, I blamed God for drafting me. I told Him He would need to find "another donkey" to carry this city burden; it was messing up my theology on submission and causing distress all around me.

Little by little I began to back off from going to the city. The prayer walks were no longer several times a week, the visits to the Drop In Center (the homeless day shelter run by Community Action) became less frequent. I felt embarrassed and ashamed my home church did not feel the need to be a part of what He had called me to do. Somewhere in my heart I had made a decision I was backing out on God and would resume a normal life (if that was even possible). About 6 weeks later I found myself in a limbo state of numbness. All "the brew ha-ha" that was happening because of this burden was exhausting and confusing.

I escaped for a weekend conference in Connecticut hoping to get some relief and to chill out. I was having a wonderful time worshiping the Lord when all of a sudden on the overhead screen behind the words was a scene of the Good Samaritan caring for the wounded man. I fell apart emotionally, I hit the floor under the pews in a puddle of tears as I sobbed "God please, I can't do this, it's not working, I'm not the right one, find another donkey. I don't have the support of my church, they just don't get me. I can't make them understand and You don't seem to be doing anything about it. What other choice do I have.....I have to quit." When all of a sudden, not expecting to hear His voice God spoke loud and clear to my heart, "Get your eyes off the people, get your eyes on Me and I will feed a city through you."

Instantly I felt conviction for pulling away from the people and the city I had grown to love and pray for. After a long conversation with God I got up, blew my beak, washed my face and called Pat Dennehey at the Drop In. Pat is the director of the center and is "not yet" a professing Christian, although she considers herself spiritual and has spiritual experiences of diverse kinds, Jesus is not "her thing". Pat and I have a great relationship, she respects me and I respect her. I have on numerous occasions had the opportunity of sharing Jesus with her. She appreciates the good that we do in the city and for the sake of the people we both love we work very well together. I blubbered on the phone, "Pat please forgive me for not coming to the Drop In these past 6 weeks. I have been backing off from the mission, it's too difficult, I don't have the support I used to have, the volunteers, resources and finances just aren't there anymore. I am so embarrassed and ashamed, I feel like I have let you and the people at the Drop In down."

49

Pat's response absolutely shocked me; she scolded me in a good, God way. She said, "Marlene Yeo it isn't the volunteers, the coats, the boots or the food that you give that matters to these people, it's the love. They know you love them; they know you care about them. You put your arms around people who smell like urine and those who are HIV positive, to some of them you are the only hug they ever get. You, of all people, should know it's about the love, not what you can give them. You give them yourself and they love you!"

Needless to say I was back to being the willing donkey. I said, "Ok God I'm in, I repent for being like Jonah and trying to run. If I have only three dollars I will buy three hot dogs and feed three people. I am willing to do whatever I can with whatever I have to do whatever You want, and please God don't ever let me ever forget "it's all about the love".

After coming to that resolve it was within a very short amount of time I received prophetic words from three different people who never met me before. I will simplify what was spoken by the Spirit of the Lord for the sake of space:

•   The leadership in the church you are now in do not understand the call of God on you for inner city ministry.

•   The Lord is removing you to place you in a church that understands the "City Church" model in Revelations, many churches pastoring the city together.

•   God is going to use your husband to help make the transition but don't worry he is going to be alright.

•   He is placing you under an apostolic leader that will receive you and release you to the call of God on your life.

50

- The Lord wants to promote you because you have been loyal and faithful to those you have served under.

- God is sending you to the dream center in L.A. because He wants you to get a vision. He wants you to dream and to dream big, because He desires to use you to build a center in your city.

It's amazing to me that once you submit to the will of God He will give you the confirmation and affirmation you need to be able to face the challenges and over come the obstacles.

And so we have the prophetic word confirmed, which you do well to heed as a light that shines in a dark place, until the day dawns and the morning star rises in your hearts.
- II Peter 1:19

Fight the good fight of faith, lay hold on eternal life, to which you were also called and have confessed the good confession in the presence of many witnesses.
- I Tim 6:12

The Bible calls it a good fight, which was interesting terminology to me. Fighting to me was never a good thing; I would avoid fighting at all costs. But God wanted to fashion me as a weapon of His love that was strong and courageous. He continues teaching me to be skilled in fighting the good fight of faith.

For by You I can run against a troop, By my God I can leap over a wall. As for God, His way is perfect; the word of the LORD is proven; He is a shield to all who trust in Him. For who is God, except the LORD? And who is a rock, except our God? It is God who arms me with strength, and makes my way perfect. He makes my feet like the feet of deer, and sets me on my high places.
- Psalm 18:29-33

I have come to believe that God picks my fights.

Then the LORD said to Satan, "Have you considered My servant Job, that there is none like him on the earth, a blameless and upright man, one who fears God and shuns evil?"
- Job 1:8

Because He knows the outcome and trusts that what He has invested in me is "enough" and His intentions for me are always good believing that in the end I will have a greater revelation of who He is.

I have heard of You by the hearing of the ear, But now my eye sees You.
- Job 42:5

Biblically one can clearly see that God chooses the opponents for the fight; they are either his adversary, his people or both. The sooner we come to grips with God's means we will learn God's ways which in turn always plants us in the center of God's will.

My intention in this chapter is not to give a negative view of the church or His people but to give you the reality of the giants you too will have to overcome to step into your destiny. It all comes down to this one thing, "When our heart is pierced will we bleed forgiveness and respond to injustice against us like Jesus did?

Father forgive them for they know not what they do.
- Luke 23:34

It's the narrow way into the promises of God. I believe that this very process is one of the reasons why the roots of bitterness and un-forgiveness can find a place in the hearts of believers. We have not yet understood the cross and that we really have no right to be offended.

8. WHEN THE MISSION BECOMES YOUR MASTER

This chapter my friend is of most importance. It helps to expose how the very mission that God calls us to can become the lord of your life and actually exalt itself above the Lord of the mission. It is extremely lethal and has the potential to destroy you, your family and the mission God has called you to. I have watched many anointed, gifted Christians not finish well because of this very subtle strategy of the enemy. It feeds into the desires of the human flesh and will ensnare you in its death grip.

There are certain tell tale signs that are red lights when this deadly enemy is taking over your life. They are exhaustion, burnout, fear, insecurity, control, manipulation, lying, cheating, exaggeration, outbursts, anger, judgments, accusations, defensiveness, hiding, compromise and blame, to mention a few.

You may be asking, how does the enemy gain such access in one's life and ministry?

The answer is very simple; we give him the authority to do so. It happens when we cross the boundaries that God has set for us and we end up being driven by the mission instead of being led by the Lord of the mission. The human soul has an issue with wanting to be number one, being right, wanting its own way, and thinking we know it all. It all boils down to one word...pride, the human soul is full of it!

The bible character that comes to mind

is King Saul, he was a man chosen by God as king of Israel. He was a handsome, tall man and the Lord said:

"There is no one in all of Israel like him."
- I Samuel 10:24

When Saul was approached by Samuel regarding God choosing him he responded in humility.

"I am of the smallest of the tribes in Israel, and my family is the least of all the families of the tribe of Benjamin, why then do you speak to me like this?"
- (I Samuel 9:21)

In I Samuel 10:1-10 When Saul was anointed as commander and king, he was told that when he came into the company of prophets the Spirit of the Lord would come upon him and he would be turned into another man with a new heart.

It's amazing how a position of authority can change a person. By the end of Saul's life God said,

"I greatly regret that I have set up Saul as king, for he has turned back from following Me, and has not performed My commandments."
- (I Samuel 15:1)

Saul's heart turned away from following God. He let the mission of being king become his master instead of the Lord. His life and mission plunged into a downward spiral when he chose to disobey God. He relied on his own wisdom; he performed a priestly duty that he had no authority from God to do.

Saul cared more about being publicly honored by the prophet of the Lord than he cared about repenting for his foolish behavior.

54

He was jealous of his son Jonathan's relationship with David, he was jealous of the next generation leader's double portion anointing. He relied on his own strength and armor instead of the Lord and he allowed God's enemies to taunt God's people.

When Samuel confronted Saul for his sinful disobedience he not only denied it but had deceived himself into thinking he had actually obeyed.

And Saul said to Samuel, "But I have obeyed the voice of the LORD, and gone on the mission on which the LORD sent me, and brought back Agag king of Amalek; I have utterly destroyed the Amalekites.
- I Samuel 15:20

Throughout Saul's life as king you can track the places he chose his mission above his master and his position of authority became more important than his obedience. He misused his anointing. His life ended in defeat...he did not finish well.

It is a sad day when a Christian forgets that their anointing is a gift from God to equip them for the mission they have been called to do. We must respect the anointing and honor the Lord with it in all we do. The authority and power that comes with the anointing is entrusted to us and equips us for the purpose of representing Him well before the people we serve. It is easy to forget what we were like before the Lord graced us with the anointing of His Holy Spirit. We, like Jesus, receive anointing from the Spirit of God because we are sent on God's mission (Luke 4:1-4). It is sobering to me how a position of authority can cause a persons heart that was once humble fall into pride and away from grace to then have God say, I regret that I gave you a place of authority. I have listed several safe guards that prevent the mission from becoming your master.

- Accountability relationships that will speak truth into your life. I have been blessed by God to have strong apostolic leaders in my life who are not afraid to instruct, rebuke, and correct me. Without truth speakers we become venerable and weak. When our words, attitudes and behavior are not lining up with the character of Christ we need a good reality check from people who love us more than they love our approval.

- Help others to succeed in what God has called them to do. When success and blessing breaks out on their life and ministry rejoice and celebrate with them.

- Keep a kingdom mentality in the forefront of your mind and heart always. You and I are only His ambassadors; we must never forget He is the King of His kingdom. The tendency to think "we are the only ones" was in the disciples thinking and is in the fiber of the church today.

Now John answered Him, saying, "Teacher, we saw someone who does not follow us casting out demons in Your name, and we forbade him because he does not follow us." But Jesus said, "Do not forbid him, for no one who works a miracle in My name can soon afterward speak evil of Me. "For he who is not against us is on our side.

- Mark 9:38-40

- Intentionally schedule time away from ministry- this will not happen without a fight. Everything inside you screams "don't do it, the ministry will suffer, people will not handle things like you do....blah, blah, blah! Do it anyway, things may fall apart which only reveals the foundation is not Christ. The ministry may suffer loss..... oh well, in the kingdom of God loss is gain.

Time away allows the reality of where you and others need to grow and mature. You have to let others feel the weight of what you carry to understand how to come along side of you and serve in the mission with you. If not you will always be the one telling people what to do instead of allowing them to have the understanding for themselves of what they need to do.

I have a saying "when God is moving it reveals His glory, when He isn't it reveals our gory". As long as there is movement there is excitement, whenever there is inactivity we often come face to face with ourselves.

• Raise up others that God has sent to do the mission with you. At some point the next generation of leaders will be the legacy you leave behind to continue the assignment God gave you to do. Give a platform for them that they made finish well.

1. Teach them how to do the mission.

2. Model for them what to do.

3. Train them how to.

4. Have them do it with you.

5. Let them do it without you.

6. From a distance be available for them as they grow in their ability to manage the mission well.

• Relationships will be one of your greatest challenges when you receive an assignment from God. Some of your closest family members and friends may never "get you". They may be the very ones that oppose you the most. It is not your job to strive to convince them, it is your job to live before them in such a way that you honor the Lord while you continue to follow His leading and love them along the way.

There are two references that helped me to navigate the emotional, relational land mines that accompany a life in ministry. I Samuel chapter 25 When David sent his men to ask Nabal for his favor and for food and drink for the feast day Nabal's response was not noble instead he was dishonorable to the king. But Nabal's wife Abigail was a woman of great wisdom. She chose to honor King David and in doing so her family was saved from harm.

When Jesus was ministering in the temple his disciples came to Him saying, Lord your mother and your brothers are outside and want you to come where they are. His reply was, "whoever does the will of God is My brother My sister and mother."
- Mark 3:32-35

The bible is clear we are to honor authority and parents but not at the risk of being disobedient to the commandments and assignments from the Lord. This dear friend is what I believe to be the ultimate challenge..... to honor the Lord in our relationships and remain obedient to His call on our lives.

I have seen many a spouse and children angry with God because of a family member who had an assignment from God that was not mentored through this challenge. There are two common reactions. "God has called me and I must forsake you to answer the call, after all how can two walk together unless they agree" or "I will quit the mission to show you that you are more important to me, God will understand." Neither of these responses is right, there are no simple answers or a 10 step guide to navigating the difficult challenge. You need to have a wise mentor in your life to walk with you through the journey, a mentor that lives successfully in the balance of ministry and family.

I thank God for the mentors He placed in my life especially for Pastor Mike Servello Sr. and his son Pastor Mike Servello, Jr. from Utica, N.Y. They have healthy family and ministry relationships as well as have planted and grown a thriving successful church and ministry. Pastor Mike Sr. has successfully passed the mantle on to the next generation of leaders.

As leaders we must expect the next generation of leaders to succeed beyond us and maybe even do a better than we did. But like Saul many leaders react to the next generation of David's double portion anointing with jealousy, insecurity and fear. God help us, is it any wonder why young people leave church and take their gifting and anointing to the world.

God has given me the privilege of mentoring very gifted young men and women who have received a double portion of anointing for their generation. Several of them have experienced a season in their journey that they served under a Saul personality type leader. During that time they were wounded, confused and most found themselves bitter because of it. I have seen God restore them to ministry and fruitfulness and have been blessed by the sweet presence of Jesus that now emanates from their life.

You will know if the mission is your master when the Lord has not called or anointed you to accomplish something that He is already doing through someone else but you continue to try to make something happen in your own ability without the anointing to do it.

Over the years I have talked to numerous believers that feel called to inner city missions, they have great ideas and exude great passion. They give it their all in trying to move forward

59

with it but unfortunately with little or no success. In one of my brilliant conversation with God I was telling Him how that doesn't look good for His reputation.

I love it when He interrupts my foolish chatter and speaks a clear word to me. I felt Him speak to my heart, "I have no obligation to anything I have not started. Whatever is started in the flesh has to be maintained and sustained by the flesh."

I have learned so much from one of my greatest mentors, Dr. Doug Stringer he taught me to identify what the Lord is already doing. The synergy and blessing that I experience today would not have been possible had I continued the way things were before I met Doug. I know that Christ is the Master of this mission and long after I am gone and my name is forgotten the ministry will, not only survive the challenges of the future, it will thrive. The mission of reaching the world with the love an power of Christ, of rescuing lives is the commandment of God; not only for the city of Haverhill and the Merrimack Valley but it is a model for the church to be the tangible expression of Christ in cities through-out New England.

9. THE GOOD, THE BAD, AND THE UGLY

If you like wearing rose colored glasses and want to believe that ministry is full of fun, fame and fortune, I suggest you skip this chapter. I feel it is important to share the reality of ministry. I've had to be very selective and careful as to what I am sharing in this chapter being mindful of the possibility that it could be very hurtful to some of the people the stories are about. I will begin with the good one and move into the bad and then the ugly!

About one year after SCNE was birthed I met Pastor Rafael Najem, Senior Pastor of Community Christian Fellowship of Lowell, Massachusetts (yay! this is the good part).

A woman that I knew from his church named Sonia had invited me to a Sunday service. Although I wasn't thrilled about traveling to Lowell, being that it is two cities away from the city I am serving in, I decided to go anyway. The first message I heard Pastor Najem preach was confirmation of every prophetic word God had given me regarding the church that He was moving me to. The following week I met with Pastor and his Associate to share the vision and mission of Somebody Cares New England, after I was finished he said, "What can we do to serve you?" I was stunned by his question but found myself answering, "My two most pressing needs are to be licensed and ordained (upon leaving my former church my credentials would be terminated) and there was great need for an inner city church plant in Haverhill.

Most of the local churches were not prepared to disciple the population of people God had called me to. Their deep rooted issues and lifestyles often posed great concern and fear for most churches (of which I completely understand). Pastor's immediate response was, "let's do it". I was rather shocked that he didn't want me to serve in the church for a time of testing, have a back ground check, and call my former pastor to see the "real reason" I was leaving or request to meet my family.

I will never forget what he said when I asked him why he was so willing and quick to receive, bless and release me in the ministry, his answer was, "I know the Spirit of God and I sense His presence, you are a gift from God to this church. I have been praying for Him to send me people like you to help us reach our city. He then invited me to minister the next four weeks on Wednesday nights to teach the congregation to be missionaries to their city.

After much prayer and relationship building God called the amazing servant leader team of SCNE to plant Community Christian Fellowship (CCF Haverhill). Our mission is "Taking the Love and Power of Christ to the Streets" we launched and our first service was November 20, 2005. All I can say is "Look what the Lord has done; it is marvelous in our sight!" Our first two years of services were held in donated space of another church on Sunday afternoons from 3-5pm.

We didn't notify the newspapers but some how they found out and we ended up on the front page. They wrote a great article stating we were the first church in the history of Haverhill planted to meet the needs of the low income population, which was news to me (good stuff).

In the first year we were able to bank a majority of the tithes and offerings. The church was located on the city block that we had been prayer walking for the past four years. This block had the reputation for the highest rate of crime, prostitution and drugs in the city. We had been praying and believing the Lord to bring transformation to the block.

By the end of the second year we were asked to leave the Church we were holding services in. There were a number of reasons why but one issue in particular that caused the leaders to make the decision was there was a group of protestors in front of the church protesting the gay marriage issue and anti-Semitism. The minister thought one of the militant religious protestors was a member of CCF; the man had been seen by one of their board members at one of our services. Although it was unfortunate we were asked to leave because of it, God used it to move us into the very corner block of storefronts that we had been praying for and believing God for transformation. Interesting how God does that. The very things He puts in your heart to pray for are the very things He uses you to accomplish.

We were excited to have our own place as well as a fearful; the work that needed to be done in the storefronts to make them useful and up to code was overwhelming and the cost of rent and utilities were a huge step of faith. We also knew the spiritual dynamics surrounding this block were going to be challenging. A front page article once we moved in said, CCF church and SCNE are changing the face of religion, when most churches move out of the city to escape inner city issues, they move in and are bringing transformation to the block...yay God!!

There were a number of homeless men and women in our church that had made, what we believed to be, sincere decisions to follow Jesus. They would continuously ask us to pray that God would provide them with jobs, and housing. Some of them were waiting on SSI or SSDI or unemployment benefits. My heart would break knowing the overwhelming challenges they were facing daily. When I read Isaiah 58:6-12 I would weep for the poor and homeless and now these precious people were coming to our church. We felt that God was speaking through Isaiah 58 that He wanted to provide a home with a structured program of discipleship for them. We had classes on finances, nutrition, conflict and anger resolution, and bible. As part of their training in servant hood they volunteered four hours a week with Somebody Cares New England giving back to the community.

There was a three story apartment building being remodeled right behind the church on the same block. We had been asking the Lord for the finances to buy it, but real estate was at an all time high and the asking price was way out of our range. The couple handling the property offered us the entire house for reasonable rent. We were so excited for the opportunity. We were able to move seven of the men off the streets. Six months later we rented another 3 unit apartment house and took in five women, one of them with her young son. The plan was for each person to pay $100.00 a week (or according to income) and that would cover everything including use of washers and dryers for each house, life was good, for everyone! This was true biblical family community and God's presence was evident in making it all come together.

I will never forget that first Christmas it was so miraculous, it was their first Christmas as a family, of God that is. After about five months things slowly began to take a turn for the worse. Jobs fell through, SSI and SSDI checks were delayed in coming there was one financial challenge after another. After the first year of opening the two houses we had eaten away the money that we had saved to the tune of $26,000.

We learned a lot in that year of what not to do the next time we are in a position to help the homeless with living quarters. We would need live in, trained staff to manage the fulltime conflicts and arguments that arose daily between them. We learned through it all that that not everyone that receives Jesus wants to let go of the past and learn new ways. We learned that providing a home and sense of stability does not guarantee a better life for people and that the spiritual warfare surrounding broken lives was much more intense than any of us understood. Though they had confessed to receiving Christ, not all were willing to crucify their sin nature which caused a great deal of difficulty and pain for everyone.

Now for the bad and ugly part, of which I feel is important to share. Some of the very ones we gave the most time, energy, patience and counsel to ended up stealing from the ministry and others in the household. They were lying, cheating, using drugs or alcohol and causing such strife and contention that a spirit of confusion permeated the atmosphere.

But if you have bitter envy and self-seeking in your hearts, do not boast and lie against the truth. 15 This wisdom does not descend from above, but is earthly, sensual, demonic. 16 For where envy and self-seeking exist, confusion and every evil thing are there.
- James 3:14-16

Arguing, selfishness and bitterness had to be dealt with on a daily basis. There were two people in particular that were a danger to themselves and others, who caused such problems that we all agreed needed to leave. We had to call the police to remove one, after they became physically combative with the police they called for backup and it took five police using mace and force to physically remove them, the other left on their own accord.

Both of them tried to destroy the ministry, there was every kind of imaginable accusation said about me, my staff and the ministry that spread through the city like wildfire. It was devastating for everyone, we loved them and thought love would take care of everything.

We have a new understanding of the scriptures that speak of the ones Jesus came to serve and set free that crucified Him. We learned that bad, ugly things sometime happen even when you are doing the right thing for the right reasons. At the close of that year we shut down the housing and helped those that remained to get relocated. The good news is none of them returned to homelessness!

It is amazing to me the revelation we get from the word of a God after we walk through these kinds of experiences. I highly recommend Dr. Stingers book, "Time to Cross the Jordan". He does an outstanding job of teaching the biblical truths from the book of Nehemiah. It has greatly helped me to understand the challenges I have faced as one called by God to restore old waste places and rebuild the former foundations.

Nehemiah was a man under authority and his burden for the well being of God's people and God's name was his only motivation. Yet, he experienced accusation, confusion, conspiracy, mocking, fear, contention, distraction and the temptation to react to it all in his flesh. The enemy's intention of the opposition was to cripple Nehemiah emotionally, mentally, physically and spiritually and to stop the work of God. The adversary always targets those who are living out their faith and acting on behalf of God's kingdom purpose.

Once moving to our new storefront location God has added to the church. We now had families, elderly and business people who have a heart for the poor. We have different ethnicity, ages, former gang members and bikers, it is beautiful to watch the Lord minister to them all. Only God can take such a diverse group of people and make them His family.

10. YAH BUT...

        I don't know about you but I have a collection of "yah buts". It's those places in our journey with the Lord where "stuff happens" that we can't wrap our mind around, find closure to or reconcile with. It causes a wrestling in our soul and has great potential to get us stuck.....permanently. It's those bad ugly things that seem to find us even when we are minding our own business and doing the right thing. I, like you, have them and praise God over the years I have learned how to move on in spite of them.

        I will share with you some of my "yah buts" that God finally broke through with revelation from His word. I will also share some that I have filed away in my "yah but" file (which is quite full having lived over 60 years). I have learned not allow them to control me or jade my relationship with my Heavenly Father. Some of them God may never feel the need to give me understanding. I have chosen to be ok with that. It doesn't mean I like it, it means I choose to trust Him even when I don't understand the whys? I call that "but God".....I believe He has good reason and there are times and seasons in our life that, for our good, He chooses to withhold the understanding.

        I used to say, "When I get to heaven I have a lot of questions for God to answer!" Then God broke through my foolish chatter and revealed through His word.

Beloved, now we are children of God; and it has not yet been revealed what we shall be, but we know that when He is revealed, we shall be like Him, for we shall see Him as He is.
- I John 3:2

        All of the questions that don't get answered here on earth will not matter once we see Him face to face.

I constantly make the choice not to waste time, energy and thoughts on the things I don't get so I can give the necessary time, energy and thoughts to the things I need to be faithful with now. Nothing zaps your strength like living in the land of "yah buts".

One of the "yah buts" I wrestled with God about was death. As a new Christian my husband and I were attending the same church as a guy we knew in high school, he and his wife had a little girl named Rachel. At about 18 months of age she died in her crib. When I found out the news I SCREAMED at God, "I thought I could trust you with my children, I will never trust you, not with my children or anyone I love."

I am so glad He understands our foolish blabber spoken out of fear and anger. He was so kind and wonderful to give me a dream shortly after Rachel's death. I saw her lying dead in her crib in a darkened room. Suddenly the door opens and an extremely bright light radiates the room. I see Jesus and I feel paralyzed by His presence as I watched Him walk to her crib and reach His arms out to her. She opened her eyes and reached out for Him. He helps her to stand in the crib. She lifts up her arms to wrap them around His neck. I can see her face beaming with joy, she is so happy to see Him. They cuddle for a few moments and the He turns to walk out the door with her. Rachel was dressed in faded denim jeans and a little red sweater. I didn't tell anyone about the dream until several months later.

The parents were moving from the apartment she died in, the pain was unbearable for them to live there. I helped them move and as I was unwrapping pictures wrapped in newspaper I unwrapped one that shocked me as I broke out in a flood of tears. It was a colored pencil sketch of Jesus with a little girl that looked like Rachel; she was dressed in faded denim jeans and a little red sweater. She was hugging His neck as He was cuddling her; she had that big smile on her face that I saw in the dream. I tried to hide what was happening to me but Rachel's mother came into the room and saw me.

Being concerned she asked me what was wrong so I told her about the dream.

She said someone had bought that picture several months before Rachel died because it looked so much like her. The day that she died she had on faded jeans and a little red sweater. I told her how God had comforted me with the dream and that He had revealed to me through it that Rachel (whose name means Lamb of God) belonged to Him; she entered into joy unspeakable and absolute peace. The same peace God desires to give to those separated from her.

God understands being separated from the ones He loves. That's why He sent Jesus to be the bridge for us to be reconciled in our relationship with Him. He crossed over into our world so we can cross over into His. I thank God for the cross! One day we will know that same joy being reunited with the Lord and our loved ones.

Walking through that painful experience has given me the courage to walk through many more tragic losses of children and adults that I have loved deeply. I, like Job, have learned to trust the Lord not only with their life but through their death.

The Lord gives and the Lord takes away, blessed be the name of the Lord.
- Job 1:21

And as David wrote in Psalm 23:

Yea, though I walk through the valley of the shadow of death I will fear no evil, thy rod and thy staff they comfort me.

The sooner we come to grips with the fact that we are not in control of life or death the sooner we can relax and trust that our Heavenly Father has it all under His control. Our children and loved ones all belong to Him. They are on loan to us for a season of time that has been determined in the great book in heaven.

...our days are numbered by the Lord.
- Psalm 139:16

Another "yah but" that used to send me into a downward spiral of self pity and despair was "If I am doing the right stuff why don't things turn out the way I hoped, believed or planned. Why wasn't I getting the results or fruit that others got or that it appeared to me they were getting? Why when I try so hard do I end up so disappointed? But God breaks through my foolishness with His word again...Oh Halleluiah!!!

...and some having died never seeing the promise knew that there was a greater promise.
- Hebrews 11:13

Some things are appointed to happen after we die...many artists, authors, inventors and missionaries never enjoyed the fruit of their labors while alive but after they passed on their lives and their work impacts hundreds, thousands or millions of people.

"...if indeed we suffer with Him, that we may also be glorified together. For I consider that the sufferings of this present time are not worthy to be compared with the glory which shall be revealed in us."
- Romans 8:17-18

70

There are many things I just don't understand, like, how is it we say that we know and love Him and can be so unforgiving to others? How do we manage to judge others harshly and critically, while we want understanding and mercy for ourselves?

When Jesus returns the word tells us He is coming back for a church without spot, wrinkle or blemish...how is He ever going to accomplish what looks to be impossible?

What is the Lord going to do about the injustice of abortion as over 60 million innocent babies' blood cries out? What is He going to do about corrupt political and church leaders? What is He going to do about the injustice and cruelty against children from the very parents that gave them life? What about men who father children but deny them nurture, provision and protection? My only resolve with my many questions is....but God!

The bible says in this life we will have tribulation, tragedy, famine and darkness.

For the time has come for judgment to begin at the house of God; and if it begins with us first, what will be the end of those who do not obey the gospel of God?
- I Peter 4:17

God is just and He will bring justice.... not when we think or hope for it to come. In the meantime he is merciful and desires that none should perish....what a Father!

Then Cain went out from the presence of the Lord and dwelt in the land of Nod on the east of Eden.
- Genesis 4:16

My heart breaks for those who refuse to trust Him, living in the limbo land of "Nod". Refusing to move forward because of "yah buts." My prayer for you is that the Lord will one day break through and reveal His goodness to you through a dream, a prophetic word or some other miraculous sign...but if that doesn't happen that you will choose to be ok and trust Him because He is God!

One of my favorite bible characters is Job. He endured tremendous suffering, losses, pain and confusion because he was righteous and yet he did not sin against God or against his "comforters". I love what he says at the end of the book when he concludes:

I had heard of you through the hearing of my ears, but now I see you.

- Job 42:5

That's what it is all about seeing Him and being transformed into His likeness through the journey called life.

My advice to you that I give to myself...in light of eternity it really doesn't matter that we know the why's, take the "yah buts" put them the "yah but" file and get on with your life. Your family needs you, the church needs you, the world needs you, you're wasting precious time when you could be doing something of value for the kingdom!

11. HE IS GOOD ALL THE TIME

I am excited about this chapter...it's all about His goodness, faithfulness and mercy.

I am going to share a few of the miracles He has done in my life, the ministry of SCNE and CCF of Haverhill. God rocks my world, when you think you are sacrificing for Him, He has ways of blessing you beyond any sacrifices you have made for His kingdom. It always outweighs anything you can attain or have on your own.

I made reference in chapter seven "These are Your People" about the prophetic word that God was going to use my husband to help make the transition from my former church to into the new place God had for me.

In July of 1999 we had moved into my dream house, it was absolutely mind blowing, above and beyond anything I could have asked or imagined. Since 1985 I had been praying for the Lord to move us closer to the church we had attended over 20 years (it was an hour round trip before the move) I felt on numerous occasions the Lord speak that He was going to build us a house. Sure enough it was a brand new house; we bought it in the second week of construction. I got to pick out everything....it was truly a dream house. You could almost say we moved from a shack to a mansion. In the later part of the second year of living in my dream my husband Harry had a heart attack, he was air lifted by helicopter to Boston for emergency surgery. The Dr's words were "10 minutes later and you would have been picking out a stone for him". Once home and beginning recovery he realized our dream home was just too big and too much to take care of. He wanted to sell and move. I was DEVASTATED, this was my dream come true.

How could Harry and God be doing this to me!

To say the least this was one of those "yah buts"! I felt the Lord reminding me of the word that the transition was going to be assisted by my husband and I praise God for the encouragement God had given that he was going to be alright (he survived the heart attack and now I was ready to kill him).

This was all in the same time frame of the difficult relational issues that were happening surrounding the call to serve in Haverhill. My husband said it would be a great time for a new start, a new beginning for everyone. I am so blessed to have a husband who supports me in my calling. He has sacrificed greatly in releasing me to ministry. Although I work very hard to keep balance with family and the work of the ministry it is a challenge.

When I left my full time paid position from my former church it was a financial sacrifice on him because I had been contributing to the household expenses as well as taking care of everything I would need for the house and myself. I explained to him that being a Somebody Cares missionary I would not get paid for serving. His response was "I know it's your passion and I support you in your decision". His only concern for me was that I would have to adjust my lifestyle to accommodate my new financial status.

After meeting with the elders to discuss the transition it was a matter of weeks before our house sold in April 2004 and 11 rooms of stuff was packed ready to go.... where, we didn't know. We ended up putting everything in storage except for basic necessities and moved into a tiny 5 room apartment looking over the river, I called it my summer home on the river. We lived there from April- September 2004. Looking for a home in Haverhill, Massachusetts was discouraging...I was spoiled in our last home. In New Hampshire you can purchase twice the house for half the money. Everything we looked at in our price range needed work, was too small, smelled like mold... yada, yada, yada.

During our search I was standing in the one person size galley kitchen in our tiny apartment and I prayed. "Lord it is no sacrifice what I have given up, like Abraham with his son...it all belongs to you to you anyway, the Lord gives and the Lord takes away blessed be the name of the Lord. But one thing I ask God, and it's not for a big beautiful house, I want Your authority and anointing for the city of Haverhill You sent me to; to set at liberty those that are bruised, open the prison doors and let the oppressed go free. To see deliverance, miracles and transformation manifested in the city streets and that Your name would be known and glorified!

September 6th we moved into our new beautiful home...I have not suffered one bit moving to this new house. As a matter of fact everyone that comes to visit says the same thing. "I thought your other house was amazing, this one exceeds beyond it in every way". How does the Lord do that? Miraculous, amazing, incredible, not only is our mortgage less but our taxes are half what they were in New Hampshire. As Matt 19:29 says, I have received one hundred fold in this life!

And for the rest of the story about my prayer for authority, the first month after moving in our new home the newspapers contacted me and wrote a profile about me upon moving to Haverhill announcing to the whole city I was sent to Haverhill on a mission. That's not all, very dear friends Dr. Gene and Sandy Heacock who had served on the founding board of directors for SCNE moved to Ohio for a season. Gene called me from Ohio to let me know that during their transition he bought the original seal of the city of Haverhill from a man in western Massachusetts who makes seals for cities. Gene's words, knowing nothing of my prayer, were "when I saw it I knew the Lord wanted you to have it as a reminder that He has given you authority in the city of Haverhill as a sent one." WOW WEE....my life is full of miraculous stories just like that, isn't God good?

12. AMAZING LOVE

One night I had a dream. I was a candy striper in a hospital. My job was to deliver flowers and run errands for the patients. As I approached this one room there were several medical professionals trying to calm a crazy lady. I stood outside the door hearing her screams for someone to help. She was angry, full of rage and had amazing physical strength. After several minutes trying to physically restrain her they gave her a shot of something that sedated her. I stood outside the door as she continued screaming for help and I wept. After she calmed they left so I went in to her room. I couldn't see her face but I knew from the color of her skin and her broken English she was Hispanic.

She was sitting on the edge of her bed, exhausted from the fight and numb from the meds, she said to me, "Please give me something for the pain". I told her, "I have no authority to give you any medication but I do have something for you. I wrapped my arms around her and hugged her. Through the open back of her hospital gown I could feel safety pins all over her back that had pierced her. My heart was wrenched with sadness, the pain she must have been suffering had to be gruesome for her to allow someone to do such a thing to her. As my hands felt the wounds on her flesh, I felt a release of the Lord's love and compassion for her. After a few brief moments I stepped back, not knowing what to expect and she was glowing with a radiant smile of peace and joy. She asked, "What just happened to me, I have no pain and for the first time in my life I feel love?"

Several months later while serving at the Drop In on a Monday holiday in came this crazy Puerto Rican girl ranting and raving, looking for a fight, for attention of any kind, she was high on cocaine. For what ever reason every time she saw me she would go off about "them loco Christians here again", her nick name was "fire cracker". She was more like the grand finally at the 4th of July fireworks.

After several months of loving her, showing patience and kindness to her, she began to trust me. Finally one day she opened up her heart to receive Christ. I asked her why she was so aggressive toward the "loco Christians" her answer was sobering. She said, "A lot of Christians think they are going to just walk in here acting like they care about us only to find a few months down the road they quit on us... they don't have any guts. I was testing you to see what you were made of....I had to see if you really cared."

I mentored her for about 4 months when she realized she needed to go to detox and had to get out of Haverhill to get clean. The day I brought her to the detox center she asked me to pick up her one and only bag of belongings she owned at the shelter. The staff person wouldn't give me the bag without first dumping everything out to see what was in it, to make sure she wasn't stealing anything from the shelter. At the very bottom of the bag was a tiny Puerto Rican flag made out of little colored beads and safety pins. As I stood there with the pins in my hand I had an epiphany, this was the dream, Annette was the crazy Puerto Rican and God had healed her pain...WOW...isn't God good to let me be a part of His dream to reach people. I love sharing stories about the "rescued ones" saved by the power of His great love! I have chosen just a few to share with you.

PETER'S STORY

I knew who Peter was; I had seen him on several occasions in the city. Peter was raised

78

in New York City, he became a gang member by the time he was 13. He lived a life of pain in his home and on the streets. In effort to escape his pain he started on a journey to Canada but somehow ended up in Haverhill. By the time I met Peter he was an alcoholic that had a liver transplant.

In his later years he married, he had finally found the love of his life....three years after they married she died of cancer. Overcome with grief and sorrow he could no longer cope with life, he saw no reason to live. He had become a recluse sitting in the darkness of his apartment day in and day out. One Sunday morning he woke up and decided, "This is the day I will go to Plug's pond and hang myself." He packed his rope in a back pack and began his journey several miles to end his life. His travel brought him by the front door of CCF just at the time service was starting. Some of the leaders were out on the side walk greeting people when Peter was walking by.

As he was warmly greeted and invited to join the service, his is testimony is, "Something gripped my heart and I knew I needed to go in. As I sat there through the worship and message I sensed a peace that I have never known. I felt loved and wanted here, I had never felt that in any church I had ever been in before". During that service one of the ministry team had a prophetic word of encouragement for Peter. She said, "The Lord calls you faithful, you are a faithful man and the Lord is going to bless you for your faithfulness."

Like I said before, I knew of Peter and faithful was not the word that would come to my mind when I saw him. He was depressed, disheveled and undone. But thank God, the Lord sees beyond where we are into where we are meant to be. Just like the bible character Peter who was like a reed blowing in the wind, Jesus called him a "rock".

Today Peter is one of the most faithful dedicated servants at both Somebody Cares and CCF Haverhill along with Ken and Maureen. These are the beautiful people that the Lord has rescued from a life of pain and despair. They are among the faithful ones that help to keep our doors open daily to meet the critical needs of the people we serve every day.

Peter's powerful testimony has encouraged many. I have brought him to other Church's when asked to share the vision of S.C.N.E. He speaks at our block parties sharing his testimony with over a thousand people. He translates for us "white folk" as we serve our Hispanic community together. Peter, among many others, are who make every challenge worth it all! I can't imagine doing anything else in life.

Pastor Jude Fouquier has been used by the Spirit of the Lord to give me numerous prophetic words of encouragement. For the purpose of this story I will tell you some of what was spoken many years ago. He said I would one day have my own TV show of which through an amazing series of events (which is another story) we have now been on the local cable TV since April of 2007.

I have had the opportunity of hosting people who have incredible testimonies of what the Lord had done in their lives through Somebody Cares. People from all walks of life all over the city tell me how much they love the show and are glad we share with them what the ministry is doing not only in Haverhill but the Merrimack Valley region.

Another time Pastor Jude under the anointing of the Holy Spirit belts out right in the middle of ministering to over 1,000 young people at the Generation Conference, "Marlene Yeo the Lord is giving you a breaker anointing of healing for the mentally ill. He is going to use you to set the captives free and restore their mind." I refer to that word here because I hosted Peter and Sharon (another volunteer) as guests one month on the Somebody Cares TV show. Their stories have touched thousands of people hearts.

Sharon's testimony is that she was the youngest child in the Boston children's hospital to be diagnosed as having a nervous breakdown. Since coming to know Christ and finding love and acceptance the Lord has healed her. Her Doctor has told her she no longer needs her psych meds. She has been declared emotionally and mentally healthy.

KEN'S STORY

Kenny was a hopeless, distressed suicidal man. He had suffered a life of violent sexual and physical abuse. He had joined the Navy looking for a place to belong. After completing his duty serving he tried to find a wife that he could build a life with to no avail. He was diagnosed with several mental and emotional disorders. Ken considered himself to be the most rejected and unlovable of all men, he felt he had no reason to live. His RN visited him several times a week to keep him on track with his meds and check up on his eating and personal care. She encouraged him to try attending CCF church services in hopes of him finding a church home he could belong to. He was afraid to come, his personal care habits were "a bit" odd and he was afraid to be rejected.

But God had a plan for Kenny's life and finally won him over. Ken was received with open arms and big hugs and has been a part of the church ever since. He is a dedicated volunteer with Somebody Cares New England and serves faithfully in CCF. God has done amazing miracles in Ken. He has one of the most tender hearted men in the ministry, all the children love

Mr. Ken and Mr. Ken loves all the kids!

MAUREEN'S STORY

When I met Maureen she was a middle age homeless woman who was barely existing in the extreme hardship she had to cope with. Although she was never an addict she called the homeless wet shelter for addicts her home which provided a tiny room with bunk beds that slept 35 men and women together. The shelter allowed their "guests" in at 5 pm and they had to leave the building by 7 am. Although Haverhill is blessed to have several outreach services that provide some type of day shelter and food. They haven't coordinated with the times and needs of the homeless. She lived in a constant state of fear and had completely closed herself off from most all human interaction.

Maureen had lost her parents many years before and had suffered a break down. She walked the streets from 7 am-5pm winter, spring, summer and fall, rain, snow extreme heat and freezing temperatures. On several occasions I tried to connect with her but she would just look at me and smile and mumble something that could not be understood. She lived in her own private world of pain and no one could reach her, or so they said! Until one day...I heard she was in the hospital in critical condition. I went to her room to visit her, the social worker; a pleasant but very professional woman was with her when I arrived. I asked her what the status on Maureen was and of course she responded professionally, "I am not at liberty to discuss with you regarding Maureen's condition.

I looked into Maureen's frightened eyes and to my utter amazement she said, "Oh that is Pastor Marlene Yeo, she is my pastor, she can know anything she wants. I have her as my proxy on my admission form." To both the so-

82

cial worker and to my shock....she seemed to be cognitive for the first time in all the years I had known her. Her social worker then shared the outcome is not expected to be good, she was critical and there wasn't much hope for change. After the social worker left I prayed for Maureen to be healed and cried out to God for His loving kindness to kiss her with the kisses of His love.

Within one year's time, the Lord moved in miraculous ways. Maureen had not only fully recovered she was moved from the shelter into a group home with proper medical care for her specific needs. She started receiving SSDI, participating in group activities, sharing in household responsibilities including meal planning, grocery shopping and cooking. Only those who knew her could see what a miracle this was. Before the end of that first year her social worker determined she was now ready to live independent in her own place...Are you kidding me?

We moved her into her own, beautiful, bright, sunny, happy place! She was beyond overjoyed....she was in shock and awe! Spending her first night alone, after 15 years, now in her own home had the potential to cause her great anxiety and alarm. When I asked her if she would be ok all alone she smiled and said, "Oh...I am not alone, He is with me". To this day I still feel tears well up as I write about Maureen's journey to wholeness.

About 18 months later, it just so happen, the social worker that I met in Maureen's room that day in the hospital came to the Somebody Cares outreach center to volunteer with her son who was planting a community garden for SCNE food pantry for his Eagle Scout project. As I showed them around the facility we came to the kitchen where Maureen was volunteering, she was astounded when she saw her and said, "Maureen is that you? You look so different, you look wonderful! How are you doing"? Maureen smiled and said, "Ever since Pastor Marlene Yeo came to my room at the hospital I knew I had a reason to live".

Nobody...nobody...nobody could EVER convince me there is no God or that He doesn't care! Maureen is living proof to the medical profession, social services, skeptics and the world there is a God and His Name is Jesus!

13. A FUTURE AND A HOPE

I can hardly wait to see what the future holds for both ministries, SCNE and CCF. We have built strong relational bridges of trust and serving alongside agencies, organizations and churches that are serving the population of people we are called to serve.

I had requested to speak before the City Council on a building code issue and received commendations from many of the city councilmen but special words of praise from a former Mayor and Detective. They stated the since the church and SCNE had moved into the city block known as the former "Bannon's Spa" the block is cleaned up, the crime rate has dropped and some of the former users are now giving back to the community volunteering though the ministry. The Detective said, "There is a large showing of support for your ministry here tonight that I would like the cameramen to get for the TV audience". He went on to say, "I personally can attest to the transformation of the lives of some of the folks here tonight. The city appreciates all you do to help the citizens of Haverhill, keep up the good work."

At the time of the writing of this book we are trusting the Lord to miraculously preserve the "first church" that was built in the city of Haverhill. It is located on Main Street directly across from City Hall. The church has parking, green space, an amazing commercial kitchen, dining hall with a stage and the sanctuary seats over 200 people. It has been for sale for many years. The asking price was over one million dollars, we knew very well it was not property that we could afford...but... we prayed and believed that God would preserve the covenant our fore fathers made with Him when they dedicated the building to the glory of God. And if it was meant for us to own....He would make a way.

After some time of it being on the market there was an offer made from Burger King. They wanted to knock the church down and build a fast food drive through. We prayed petitioning the Lord to preserve the church as a part of our Godly heritage and for the building to be used once again for His glory.

During the time this was going on we were hosting our annual Somebody Cares "Bless the City" summer outreach. We offer youth and families three days of teaching with hands on training preparing them to be missionaries to their own city. During the event we teach about the importance of knowing the history of your city to better determine God's destiny for the city and to pray into God's original design. We teach Christians how to research, do prayer walks, and random acts of kindness offering to pray for people to receive forgiveness and experience the love of Christ.

As part of their training we taught on the history of the "first church", walked the property and declared Jesus Christ Lord over the land and building and that Burger King is the wrong king, Jesus is King. We prayed for His Kingdom to be established in this historic church that our forefathers dedicated to God.

Crazy as it sounds...that afternoon's headlines in the local paper read...Historic church is not the place for a Burger King. The small print went on to read, the right fit would be for a church like Community Christian Fellowship Pastored by Marlene Yeo that reaches out to help the citizens of Haverhill. Talk about timing...what a great object lesson it was for those learning about praying into destiny. I will cover more on this in greater detail in my sequel book, "He is looking for a

Donkey"...to ride into your city.

Although we have not been the ones to purchase the "first church" (as of yet) I am thrilled to say it is still a church and not a Burger King. The Lord opened the door for us to purchase property on 358 Washington Street in Haverhill to house both the SCNE outreach center and CCF Haverhill church. The property was built as a funeral home and through the Lord's miraculous provision of finances and resources it is no longer a place of death and sorrow; it is now a house of life and joy. Over $50,000 was donated by people who believe in the mission and vision. One woman from another state donated $30,000 and another woman that was homeless that we provided housing for in the discipleship house donated $1000. God's will is God's bill!

Since purchasing the property it has provided us the space to give literally tons of food to thousands of people through the SCNE food pantry. Yup...just like God said, "get your eyes off of people, get your eyes on Me and I will feed a city through you."

I know the Lord has only just begun what He desires to do here in Haverhill, the Merrimack Valley and New England. I am so grateful that He has allowed an ordinary person like me to be a small part of seeing His dream come to pass.

When Pastor Mike Servello Sr. came to preach at the launch service for CCF Haverhill, he said to me, "Marlene because you are willing to care for the ones nobody wants; God is going to bring you the ones everybody wants." I am grateful for the favor of the Lord, the relationships and networks that God has blessed us with, it is truly amazing.

Does your heart yearn for something more than the ritual and tradition of Christianity? For those who feel called to live a life-style of sharing the gospel with "not yet" believers, maybe God is calling you to be a part of a global prayer, compassion, evangelism movement that is "bigger than yourself".

For more information on SCNE:
web: www.somebodycaresNE.org
email: office@somebodycaresNE.org
Mailing address: 358 Washington Street,
Haverhill, Mass 01832

**For more information on
Community Christian Fellowship
(CCF Haverhill):**
web: www.ccfhaverhill.com
email: office@ccfhaverhill.com
Mailing address: 358 Washington Street,
Haverhill, Mass 01832

35504295R00051

Made in the USA
Middletown, DE
06 October 2016